THE ASIAN KITCHEN

A Delightful Collection of Chinese, Korean, and Baking Bread Recipes for Your Family Cookbook

ORDU MAXWELL

Contents

The Asian kitchen

The Asian kitchen

The Asian kitchen

The Asian kitchen

Introduction:

Are you ready to embark on a culinary journey through the vibrant flavors of Asia? Look no further than "The Asian Kitchen: A Delightful Collection of Chinese, Korean, and Baking Bread Recipes for Your Family Cookbook." This cookbook is your gateway to an enchanting world of savory Chinese dishes, authentic Korean delicacies, and delectable baked goods that will captivate your taste buds and bring joy to your family gatherings.

Picture yourself savoring the aromatic spices of a Chinese Kung Pao Chicken, its tender pieces of chicken coated in a tantalizing sauce, or imagine indulging in the comforting warmth of a bowl of Korean Japchae, its delicate glass noodles intermingled with colorful vegetables. Whether you're a fan of Chinese cooking, eager to explore the diverse flavors of

Korean cuisine, or simply passionate about baking bread, this cookbook has something to offer for everyone.

With "The Asian Kitchen," you can unleash your inner chef and create restaurant-quality dishes in the comfort of your own kitchen. Each recipe is carefully crafted and presented with clear step-by-step instructions, ensuring that even novice cooks can confidently prepare authentic Asian meals. No need to scour specialty stores for rare ingredients—these recipes feature readily available items that can be found in your local supermarket, making them accessible and convenient.

Prepare to immerse yourself in the culinary traditions of Asia, as "The Asian Kitchen" not only provides delicious recipes but also offers a glimpse into the rich cultural heritage behind each dish. Discover the techniques, spices, and ingredients that define Asian cuisine and

The Asian kitchen

elevate your cooking skills to new heights. Gather your loved ones, set aside some time for culinary adventures, and create lasting memories as you embark on this flavorful journey through Asia.

With "The Asian Kitchen: A Delightful Collection of Chinese, Korean, and Baking Bread Recipes for Your Family Cookbook," you hold the key to unlocking a world of culinary delights. Get ready to tantalize your taste buds, expand your culinary horizons, and bring the flavors of Asia into your home. Let the aroma of exotic spices fill your kitchen and the smiles of your loved ones light up the dining table. Are you ready to embark on this gastronomic adventure? It all starts with "The Asian Kitchen."

The Asian kitchen

Food and their recipes

Kung Pao Chicken:

Ingredients:

1 lb (450g) boneless, skinless chicken breasts, cut into bite-sized pieces

1/2 cup unsalted peanuts

2 tablespoons vegetable oil

3-4 dried red chilies

3 cloves garlic, minced

1 tablespoon fresh ginger, grated

1/2 cup diced bell peppers (assorted colors)

1/2 cup diced onion

2 tablespoons soy sauce

1 tablespoon rice vinegar

1 tablespoon hoisin sauce

1 teaspoon sugar

The Asian kitchen

1 teaspoon cornstarch, dissolved in 2 tablespoons water

Green onions, chopped (for garnish)

Preparation:

Heat the vegetable oil in a large skillet or wok over medium-high heat. Add the chicken and stir-fry until cooked through and lightly browned. Remove the chicken from the skillet and set aside.

In the same skillet, add the peanuts and dried red chilies. Stir-fry for 1-2 minutes until the peanuts are toasted and the chilies are fragrant. Remove them from the skillet and set aside.

In the same skillet, add the garlic and ginger. Stir-fry for 30 seconds until fragrant. Add the bell peppers and onion, and stir-fry for another 2-3 minutes until they begin to soften.

The Asian kitchen

Return the cooked chicken to the skillet. In a small bowl, whisk together the soy sauce, rice vinegar, hoisin sauce, sugar, and cornstarch mixture. Pour the sauce over the chicken and vegetables, stirring constantly until the sauce thickens and coats everything evenly.

Remove from heat and garnish with toasted peanuts, dried red chilies, and chopped green onions. Serve hot with steamed rice.

The Asian kitchen

Bulgogi (Korean Marinated Beef):

Ingredients:

1 lb (450g) beef sirloin, thinly sliced

1/4 cup soy sauce

2 tablespoons brown sugar

2 tablespoons sesame oil

2 cloves garlic, minced

1 tablespoon grated pear

1 tablespoon grated onion

1 teaspoon grated ginger

2 green onions, thinly sliced

Sesame seeds (for garnish)

Preparation:

In a bowl, combine soy sauce, brown sugar, sesame oil, minced garlic, grated pear, grated onion, grated ginger, and half

The Asian kitchen

of the sliced green onions. Mix well until the sugar is dissolved.

Add the beef slices to the marinade, ensuring each piece is well coated. Cover the bowl and refrigerate for at least 1 hour, allowing the flavors to meld.

Preheat a grill or a skillet over medium-high heat. Cook the marinated beef in batches for 2-3 minutes per side or until desired doneness.

Remove from heat and garnish with sesame seeds and remaining sliced green onions. Serve with steamed rice and kimchi for a complete Korean meal.

Artisanal Herb and Cheese Bread:

Ingredients:

3 1/2 cups bread flour

2 teaspoons instant yeast

1 1/2 teaspoons salt

2 tablespoons olive oil

1 1/4 cups warm water (around 110°F/43°C)

1 cup grated cheddar cheese

1/4 cup chopped fresh herbs (such as rosemary, thyme, and basil)

Preparation:

In a large mixing bowl, combine bread flour, instant yeast, and salt. Make a well in the center and add olive oil and warm water. Stir with a wooden spoon until a sticky dough forms.

The Asian kitchen

Transfer the dough to a floured surface and knead for about 5-7 minutes until smooth and elastic. Place the dough in a greased bowl, cover with a clean kitchen towel, and let it rise in a warm place for 1-2 hours or until doubled in size.

Preheat the oven to 425°F (220°C). Punch down the dough to release any air bubbles and transfer it to a lightly floured surface. Flatten the dough into a rectangle and sprinkle the grated cheese and chopped herbs evenly over the surface.

Roll the dough tightly from one end to form a loaf shape. Pinch the ends to seal. Place the loaf on a parchment-lined baking sheet and let it rise for an additional 30 minutes.

Bake the bread in the preheated oven for 25-30 minutes or until golden brown and sounds hollow when tapped on the bottom. Allow it to cool on a wire rack before slicing and serving.

Enjoy the delectable flavors of these homemade dishes from "The Asian

The Asian kitchen

Kitchen" and create unforgettable meals for your family and loved ones.

Mapo Tofu:

Ingredients:

1 tablespoon vegetable oil

1 tablespoon Sichuan peppercorns

2 tablespoons fermented black beans, rinsed and minced

3 cloves garlic, minced

1 tablespoon minced ginger

1/2 lb (225g) ground pork

2 tablespoons doubanjiang (spicy bean paste)

1 tablespoon soy sauce

1 tablespoon Shaoxing wine

1 cup chicken or vegetable broth

1 tablespoon cornstarch, dissolved in 2 tablespoons water

The Asian kitchen

1 package (14 oz/400g) soft tofu, cut into small cubes

2 green onions, chopped (for garnish)

Preparation:

Heat the vegetable oil in a wok or large skillet over medium-high heat. Add the Sichuan peppercorns and toast for 1-2 minutes until fragrant. Remove the peppercorns and set them aside.

In the same wok, add the minced fermented black beans, garlic, and ginger. Stir-fry for about 30 seconds until aromatic. Add the ground pork and cook until browned.

Stir in the doubanjiang, soy sauce, and Shaoxing wine. Mix well to combine all the flavors.

Pour in the chicken or vegetable broth and bring to a simmer. Add the dissolved cornstarch and stir until the sauce thickens.

Gently add the tofu cubes and cook for an additional 2-3 minutes, being careful not to break the tofu. Remove from heat and garnish with chopped green onions. Serve hot with steamed rice.

The Asian kitchen

Bibimbap (Korean Mixed Rice Bowl):

Ingredients:

2 cups cooked short-grain rice

1 tablespoon sesame oil

1 cup thinly sliced beef (can use ribeye or sirloin)

1 cup julienned carrots

1 cup julienned zucchini

1 cup bean sprouts

1 cup spinach, blanched and squeezed dry

4 eggs, fried sunny-side up

2 tablespoons gochujang (Korean chili paste)

1 tablespoon soy sauce

1 tablespoon toasted sesame seeds

The Asian kitchen

Salt, to taste

Vegetable oil, for cooking

Preparation:

Heat vegetable oil in a skillet over medium-high heat. Add the beef slices and cook until browned. Drizzle with soy sauce and stir until coated. Remove from heat and set aside.

In the same skillet, add a little more vegetable oil if needed. Stir-fry the carrots and zucchini separately until slightly tender. Season with a pinch of salt. Remove from heat and set aside.

Blanch the bean sprouts in boiling water for 1-2 minutes. Drain and season with salt and sesame oil. Set aside.

In a small bowl, mix together gochujang and sesame oil to make a sauce.

Assemble the bibimbap: Divide the cooked rice into four bowls. Arrange the beef, carrots, zucchini, bean sprouts,

The Asian kitchen

spinach, and fried eggs on top of the rice in separate sections. Drizzle the gochujang sauce over the ingredients. Sprinkle with toasted sesame seeds.

To eat, mix all the ingredients together thoroughly, breaking the egg yolk and allowing it to coat the rice and vegetables. Enjoy the flavorsome medley of textures and tastes!

These recipes from "The Asian Kitchen" will take your taste buds on a flavorful journey through Chinese, Korean, and bread baking delights. Enjoy preparing these dishes for your family and friends, and savor the wonderful flavors of Asian cuisine.

The Asian kitchen

General Tso's Chicken:

Ingredients:

1 lb (450g) boneless, skinless chicken thighs, cut into bite-sized pieces

1/4 cup cornstarch

2 tablespoons vegetable oil

3 cloves garlic, minced

1 tablespoon fresh ginger, grated

1/4 cup soy sauce

2 tablespoons hoisin sauce

2 tablespoons rice vinegar

2 tablespoons honey

1 teaspoon sesame oil

1/2 teaspoon red pepper flakes (optional)

1/4 cup water

2 green onions, chopped (for garnish)

Sesame seeds (for garnish)

The Asian kitchen

Preparation:

In a bowl, coat the chicken pieces with cornstarch, ensuring they are evenly coated. Set aside.

Heat vegetable oil in a large skillet or wok over medium-high heat. Add the coated chicken pieces and cook until golden brown and crispy. Remove the chicken from the skillet and set aside.

In the same skillet, add minced garlic and grated ginger. Stir-fry for about 30 seconds until fragrant.

In a small bowl, whisk together soy sauce, hoisin sauce, rice vinegar, honey, sesame oil, red pepper flakes (if using), and water. Pour the sauce into the skillet and bring it to a simmer.

The Asian kitchen

Add the cooked chicken back into the skillet and toss until it is evenly coated in the sauce. Cook for an additional 2-3 minutes until the sauce thickens and caramelizes.

Remove from heat and garnish with chopped green onions and sesame seeds. Serve hot with steamed rice.

The Asian kitchen

Kimchi Fried Rice:

Ingredients:

2 cups cooked rice (preferably day-old)

1 cup kimchi, chopped

1/4 cup kimchi juice

4 slices bacon, chopped

1/2 cup diced onion

1/2 cup frozen peas and carrots

2 tablespoons soy sauce

1 tablespoon sesame oil

2 green onions, chopped (for garnish)

1 fried egg (optional, for serving)

Preparation:

Heat a large skillet or wok over medium heat. Add chopped bacon and cook until

The Asian kitchen

crispy. Remove the bacon from the skillet and set aside.

In the same skillet, add diced onion and frozen peas and carrots. Stir-fry for a few minutes until the vegetables are heated through and the onion becomes translucent.

Add chopped kimchi to the skillet and stir-fry for another 1-2 minutes.

Push the kimchi mixture to one side of the skillet and add the cooked rice to the other side. Break up any clumps of rice with a spatula and stir-fry for a few minutes.

Pour kimchi juice, soy sauce, and sesame oil over the rice. Mix everything together until the rice is well coated and heated through.

Remove from heat and garnish with chopped green onions and the crispy bacon. Top with a fried egg, if desired. Serve hot and enjoy the bold and tangy flavors of kimchi fried rice.

The Asian kitchen

These recipes from "The Asian Kitchen" will surely impress your taste buds and allow you to explore the diverse and delicious flavors of Asian cuisine. Enjoy preparing these dishes and delight in the culinary delights of Chinese, Korean, and bread baking.

Sweet and Sour Pork:

Ingredients:

1 lb (450g) pork tenderloin, cut into bite-sized pieces

1/2 cup cornstarch

Vegetable oil, for frying

1 green bell pepper, diced

1 red bell pepper, diced

1 small onion, diced

The Asian kitchen

1 cup pineapple chunks

1/4 cup ketchup

3 tablespoons rice vinegar

2 tablespoons brown sugar

1 tablespoon soy sauce

1/2 cup water

Sesame seeds, for garnish (optional)

Chopped green onions, for garnish (optional)

Preparation:

In a bowl, coat the pork pieces with cornstarch until they are evenly coated. Shake off any excess cornstarch.

Heat vegetable oil in a large skillet or wok over medium-high heat. Fry the coated pork pieces in batches until they are crispy and golden brown. Remove the pork from the skillet and drain on paper towels.

The Asian kitchen

In the same skillet, add the diced bell peppers and onion. Stir-fry for a few minutes until they are slightly tender.

In a separate bowl, whisk together ketchup, rice vinegar, brown sugar, soy sauce, and water to make the sweet and sour sauce.

Pour the sauce into the skillet with the bell peppers and onion. Stir until the sauce thickens and coats the vegetables.

Add the fried pork and pineapple chunks to the skillet. Stir everything together until the pork and pineapple are well coated in the sauce. Cook for an additional 2-3 minutes.

The Asian kitchen

Remove from heat and garnish with sesame seeds and chopped green onions, if desired. Serve hot with steamed rice.

Japchae (Korean Stir-Fried Glass Noodles):

Ingredients:

8 oz (225g) sweet potato glass noodles (dangmyeon)

2 tablespoons vegetable oil

1 lb (450g) beef sirloin, thinly sliced

2 cloves garlic, minced

1 medium carrot, julienned

1 medium onion, thinly sliced

1 red bell pepper, thinly sliced

4-5 fresh shiitake mushrooms, thinly sliced

2 cups baby spinach

2 tablespoons soy sauce

1 tablespoon sesame oil

1 tablespoon brown sugar

1 teaspoon toasted sesame seeds

Salt and pepper, to taste

Preparation:

Cook the sweet potato glass noodles according to the package instructions. Drain and set aside.

In a large skillet or wok, heat vegetable oil over medium-high heat. Add the beef slices and minced garlic. Stir-fry until the beef is cooked through. Remove the beef from the skillet and set aside.

In the same skillet, add the carrot, onion, red bell pepper, and shiitake mushrooms. Stir-fry for a few minutes until the vegetables are tender.

The Asian kitchen

Add the cooked glass noodles to the skillet, along with the baby spinach. Stir-fry until the spinach wilts.

In a small bowl, whisk together soy sauce, sesame oil, brown sugar, salt, and pepper. Pour the sauce over the noodles and vegetables. Mix everything together until well combined.

Return the cooked beef to the skillet and toss everything together to heat through.

Remove from heat and sprinkle with toasted sesame seeds. Serve hot as a delicious and satisfying meal.

These recipes from "The Asian Kitchen" will elevate your culinary repertoire and bring the flavors of Chinese, Korean, and baking bread into your home. Enjoy the process of creating these delectable dishes and share them with your loved ones for memorable meals together.

The Asian kitchen

Kung Pao Chicken:

Ingredients:

1 lb (450g) boneless, skinless chicken breasts, cut into bite-sized pieces

1/2 cup unsalted peanuts

2 tablespoons vegetable oil

2 cloves garlic, minced

1 tablespoon fresh ginger, grated

2-3 dried red chili peppers, chopped

1/2 cup diced bell peppers (red and green)

1/2 cup diced zucchini

1/2 cup diced carrots

2 green onions, chopped (white and green parts separated)

2 tablespoons soy sauce

1 tablespoon hoisin sauce

The Asian kitchen

1 tablespoon rice vinegar

1 tablespoon cornstarch, dissolved in 2 tablespoons water

Sesame seeds, for garnish (optional)

Preparation:

In a dry skillet, toast the unsalted peanuts over medium heat until lightly browned. Remove from heat and set aside.

Heat vegetable oil in a large skillet or wok over medium-high heat. Add minced garlic, grated ginger, and chopped dried red chili peppers. Stir-fry for about 30 seconds until fragrant.

Add the chicken pieces to the skillet and cook until browned and cooked through.

The Asian kitchen

Push the chicken to one side of the skillet and add the diced bell peppers, zucchini, carrots, and white parts of the green onions. Stir-fry for a few minutes until the vegetables are tender-crisp.

In a small bowl, whisk together soy sauce, hoisin sauce, rice vinegar, and the dissolved cornstarch.

Pour the sauce into the skillet and toss everything together until well coated. Cook for an additional minute or until the sauce thickens.

Remove from heat and garnish with toasted peanuts, green parts of the green onions, and sesame seeds, if desired. Serve hot with steamed rice.

The Asian kitchen

Steamed BBQ Pork Buns (Char Siu Bao):

Ingredients:

For the dough:

2 cups all-purpose flour

1 tablespoon sugar

1 teaspoon instant yeast

1/2 cup warm water

1 tablespoon vegetable oil

For the filling:

1 cup char siu (barbecue pork), diced

1 tablespoon hoisin sauce

1 tablespoon oyster sauce

1 tablespoon soy sauce

The Asian kitchen

1 tablespoon cornstarch, dissolved in 2 tablespoons water

Preparation:

In a large bowl, combine all-purpose flour, sugar, and instant yeast. Make a well in the center and pour in warm water and vegetable oil. Stir until a sticky dough forms.

Transfer the dough to a floured surface and knead for about 5 minutes until smooth and elastic. Place the dough in a greased bowl, cover with a clean kitchen towel, and let it rise in a warm place for 1 hour or until doubled in size.

Punch down the dough and divide it into small portions. Roll each portion into a ball and flatten it into a circle using a rolling pin. Spoon a portion of the filling onto the center of each circle and gather the edges together, pinching and twisting to seal the bun.

Place the buns on parchment paper squares and arrange them in a steamer basket. Let them rest for 15 minutes.

Steam the buns over high heat for about 15 minutes or until the buns are puffed up and cooked through.

Remove from heat and serve the steamed BBQ pork buns hot as a delicious snack or appetizer.

These recipes from "The Asian Kitchen: A Delightful Collection of Chinese, Korean, and Baking Bread Recipes for Your Family Cookbook" will surely impress your family and friends with their authentic flavors and delightful taste. Enjoy the journey of creating these dishes and let the aromas and flavors transport you to the heart of Asian cuisine.

The Asian kitchen

Mapo Tofu:

Ingredients:

1 block (14 oz/400g) firm tofu, cut into small cubes

2 tablespoons vegetable oil

2 cloves garlic, minced

1 tablespoon ginger, grated

2 tablespoons doubanjiang (spicy bean paste)

1 tablespoon soy sauce

1 teaspoon Sichuan peppercorns, toasted and ground

1 cup chicken or vegetable broth

1 tablespoon cornstarch, dissolved in 2 tablespoons water

2 green onions, chopped (white and green parts)

Steamed rice, for serving

The Asian kitchen

Preparation:

Heat vegetable oil in a large skillet or wok over medium heat. Add minced garlic and grated ginger. Stir-fry for about 30 seconds until fragrant.

Add doubanjiang (spicy bean paste) to the skillet and stir-fry for another minute.

Add the tofu cubes to the skillet and gently stir to coat them with the sauce.

Pour in soy sauce and sprinkle in ground Sichuan peppercorns. Stir gently to combine.

Add chicken or vegetable broth to the skillet and bring it to a simmer. Let it cook for about 5 minutes.

The Asian kitchen

Stir in the dissolved cornstarch and continue cooking until the sauce thickens.

Remove from heat and garnish with chopped green onions. Serve hot over steamed rice.

Korean Bulgogi:

Ingredients:

1 lb (450g) beef sirloin, thinly sliced

1/4 cup soy sauce

2 tablespoons brown sugar

2 tablespoons sesame oil

2 cloves garlic, minced

1 tablespoon grated fresh ginger

2 green onions, chopped (white and green parts)

The Asian kitchen

1 tablespoon sesame seeds

1 tablespoon vegetable oil, for cooking

Steamed rice, for serving

Lettuce leaves, for wrapping (optional)

Preparation:

In a bowl, combine soy sauce, brown sugar, sesame oil, minced garlic, grated ginger, chopped green onions, and sesame seeds. Stir until well mixed.

Add the sliced beef to the marinade and toss to coat. Let it marinate for at least 30 minutes, or up to overnight in the refrigerator.

Heat vegetable oil in a skillet or grill pan over medium-high heat.

Remove the beef from the marinade and cook it in the hot skillet for 2-3 minutes per side, or until browned and cooked to your desired doneness.

The Asian kitchen

Remove from heat and let it rest for a few minutes.

Slice the cooked beef into thin strips.

Serve the bulgogi hot over steamed rice. Optionally, serve with lettuce leaves for wrapping the beef.

Enjoy the delightful flavors of these authentic Asian dishes from "The Asian Kitchen" and let them transport you to the vibrant culinary landscapes of Chinese, Korean, and baking bread.

The Asian kitchen

Japchae (Korean Glass Noodles):

Ingredients:

8 oz (225g) Korean sweet potato glass noodles

2 tablespoons vegetable oil

2 cloves garlic, minced

1 onion, thinly sliced

1 carrot, julienned

1 red bell pepper, thinly sliced

4 oz (115g) spinach

4 oz (115g) shiitake mushrooms, sliced

2 tablespoons soy sauce

1 tablespoon sesame oil

1 tablespoon sugar

1 tablespoon sesame seeds, toasted

Salt and pepper to taste

Preparation:

Cook the glass noodles according to the package instructions. Drain and rinse under cold water. Set aside.

Heat vegetable oil in a large skillet or wok over medium heat. Add minced garlic and sauté until fragrant.

Add sliced onions, julienned carrots, and sliced bell peppers to the skillet. Stir-fry for a few minutes until the vegetables are tender-crisp.

Add spinach and shiitake mushrooms to the skillet. Cook until the spinach is wilted and the mushrooms are tender.

In a small bowl, whisk together soy sauce, sesame oil, sugar, salt, and pepper. Pour the sauce over the vegetables in the skillet and stir to coat everything evenly.

The Asian kitchen

Add the cooked glass noodles to the skillet and toss to combine with the vegetables and sauce.

Cook for an additional 2-3 minutes until everything is heated through.

Remove from heat and garnish with toasted sesame seeds. Serve hot as a flavorful and nutritious dish.

The Asian kitchen

Baking Bread: Classic French

Baguette:

Ingredients:

3 1/2 cups bread flour

2 1/4 teaspoons active dry yeast

2 teaspoons salt

1 1/2 cups warm water

Cornmeal or semolina, for dusting

Preparation:

In a large bowl, combine bread flour, active dry yeast, and salt. Mix well.

Gradually add warm water to the flour mixture, stirring until a shaggy dough forms.

The Asian kitchen

Transfer the dough to a lightly floured surface and knead for about 10 minutes until smooth and elastic.

Place the dough in a greased bowl, cover with a clean kitchen towel, and let it rise in a warm place for about 1 hour or until doubled in size.

Punch down the dough and turn it out onto a lightly floured surface. Divide the dough into two equal portions.

Shape each portion into a long baguette shape, about 14-16 inches long. Place the baguettes on a baking sheet sprinkled with cornmeal or semolina.

Cover the baguettes with a clean kitchen towel and let them rise for another 30-45 minutes until puffed.

Meanwhile, preheat the oven to 475°F (245°C). Place a baking dish filled with water on the bottom rack of the oven.

Using a sharp knife or a razor blade, make diagonal slashes on the top of each baguette.

The Asian kitchen

Bake the baguettes in the preheated oven for 20-25 minutes until golden brown and crusty.

Remove from the oven and let the baguettes cool on a wire rack before slicing and serving.

Enjoy the culinary delights of Japchae and the satisfaction of baking your own classic French baguette with these recipes from "The Asian Kitchen: A Delightful Collection of Chinese, Korean, and Baking Bread Recipes for Your Family Cookbook." Happy cooking and baking!

Chinese Steamed Dumplings

(Jiaozi):

Ingredients:

For the dumpling dough:

2 cups all-purpose flour

1 cup warm water

1/2 teaspoon salt

For the filling:

1/2 lb (225g) ground pork

1 cup cabbage, finely chopped

2 green onions, finely chopped

1 clove garlic, minced

1 tablespoon soy sauce

1 tablespoon sesame oil

1 teaspoon grated fresh ginger

Salt and pepper to taste

The Asian kitchen

Preparation:

In a large bowl, combine the flour, warm water, and salt. Mix until a dough forms.

Transfer the dough to a lightly floured surface and knead for about 5 minutes until smooth and elastic. Cover with a damp cloth and let it rest for 30 minutes.

In a separate bowl, combine the ground pork, chopped cabbage, green onions, minced garlic, soy sauce, sesame oil, grated ginger, salt, and pepper. Mix well.

Divide the dough into small portions. Roll each portion into a thin circle, about 3 inches in diameter.

Place a spoonful of the filling in the center of each dough circle. Fold the dough in

The Asian kitchen

half and pinch the edges together to seal, creating a crescent shape.

Repeat the process until all the dough and filling are used.

Prepare a steamer by filling a pot with water and bringing it to a boil. Line the steamer basket with parchment paper or cabbage leaves to prevent sticking.

Arrange the dumplings in the steamer basket, leaving space between them to prevent sticking.

Place the steamer basket over the boiling water and steam the dumplings for about 15 minutes or until cooked through.

Remove the dumplings from the steamer and serve hot with soy sauce or your favorite dipping sauce.

The Asian kitchen

Korean Bibimbap:

Ingredients:

2 cups cooked short-grain rice

4 oz (115g) beef, thinly sliced

1 carrot, julienned

1 zucchini, julienned

1 cup bean sprouts

1 cup spinach

4 shiitake mushrooms, sliced

4 eggs

2 tablespoons vegetable oil

2 tablespoons soy sauce

1 tablespoon sesame oil

1 clove garlic, minced

Salt and pepper to taste

Sesame seeds, for garnish

The Asian kitchen

Gochujang (Korean red pepper paste), for serving

Heat 1 tablespoon of vegetable oil in a skillet over medium heat. Add the beef slices and cook until browned. Remove from heat and set aside.

In the same skillet, heat another tablespoon of vegetable oil. Add the carrot, zucchini, bean sprouts, spinach, and shiitake mushrooms. Sauté each vegetable separately until tender-crisp. Season with salt, pepper, and minced garlic while cooking.

In a small bowl, whisk together soy sauce and sesame oil. Pour the sauce over the cooked vegetables and toss to coat.

In a separate skillet, fry the eggs sunny-side-up or to your desired doneness.

To assemble the bibimbap, divide the cooked rice into serving bowls. Arrange

The Asian kitchen

the cooked vegetables, beef, and fried eggs on top of the rice.

Garnish with sesame seeds and serve hot with a dollop of gochujang on the side.

Mix everything together before eating to enjoy the flavors of the different ingredients.

Enjoy the delicious Chinese steamed dumplings and Korean bibimbap from "The Asian Kitchen: A Delightful Collection of Chinese, Korean, and Baking Bread Recipes for Your Family Cookbook." Happy cooking and bon appétit!

Chinese Hot and Sour Soup:

Ingredients:

4 cups chicken or vegetable broth

4 oz (115g) firm tofu, diced

1/2 cup bamboo shoots, sliced

1/4 cup wood ear mushrooms, rehydrated and sliced

2 tablespoons soy sauce

2 tablespoons rice vinegar

1 tablespoon cornstarch, dissolved in 2 tablespoons water

1 egg, lightly beaten

1 teaspoon sesame oil

2 green onions, chopped

Salt and pepper to taste

Preparation:

The Asian kitchen

In a large pot, bring the chicken or vegetable broth to a boil.

Add the diced tofu, sliced bamboo shoots, and wood ear mushrooms to the boiling broth. Cook for about 5 minutes.

In a small bowl, whisk together soy sauce, rice vinegar, and cornstarch-water mixture until smooth.

Slowly pour the soy sauce mixture into the soup while stirring continuously. Cook for another 2-3 minutes until the soup thickens slightly.

Slowly pour the beaten egg into the soup in a thin stream, stirring gently with a fork to create egg ribbons.

The Asian kitchen

Add sesame oil, chopped green onions, salt, and pepper to the soup. Stir to combine.

Remove from heat and serve hot as a comforting and flavorful soup.

The Asian kitchen

Korean Bulgogi (Grilled Marinated Beef):

Ingredients:

1 lb (450g) beef sirloin or ribeye, thinly sliced

1/4 cup soy sauce

2 tablespoons brown sugar

2 tablespoons sesame oil

2 cloves garlic, minced

1 teaspoon grated fresh ginger

1 tablespoon toasted sesame seeds

2 green onions, chopped (white and green parts)

1 tablespoon vegetable oil, for cooking

Rice, for serving

Lettuce leaves, for wrapping (optional)

The Asian kitchen

Preparation:

In a bowl, combine soy sauce, brown sugar, sesame oil, minced garlic, grated ginger, toasted sesame seeds, and chopped green onions. Mix well to make the marinade.

Add the thinly sliced beef to the marinade and toss to coat. Let it marinate for at least 30 minutes, or up to overnight in the refrigerator for a more intense flavor.

Heat vegetable oil in a skillet or grill pan over medium-high heat.

Remove the beef slices from the marinade, shaking off any excess marinade, and place them in the hot skillet. Cook for 2-3 minutes per side until browned and cooked to your desired doneness.

Remove the cooked beef from the skillet and let it rest for a few minutes.

Serve the bulgogi hot over steamed rice. Optionally, you can wrap the bulgogi in lettuce leaves for a refreshing and light meal.

Enjoy the vibrant flavors of Chinese Hot and Sour Soup and the mouthwatering Korean Bulgogi from "The Asian Kitchen: A Delightful Collection of Chinese, Korean, and Baking Bread Recipes for Your Family Cookbook." Happy cooking and enjoy your meal!

The Asian kitchen

Baking Bread: Japanese Milk Bread:

Ingredients:

2 3/4 cups bread flour

1/4 cup granulated sugar

2 teaspoons active dry yeast

1 teaspoon salt

1/2 cup warm milk

2 tablespoons unsalted butter, softened

1 egg

Egg wash (1 egg beaten with 1 tablespoon milk)

Preparation:

In a large bowl, combine bread flour, sugar, active dry yeast, and salt. Mix well.

Add warm milk, softened butter, and egg to the bowl. Stir until a soft dough forms.

The Asian kitchen

Transfer the dough to a lightly floured surface and knead for about 10 minutes until smooth and elastic.

Place the dough in a greased bowl, cover with a clean kitchen towel, and let it rise in a warm place for about 1 hour or until doubled in size.

Punch down the dough and turn it out onto a lightly floured surface. Divide the dough into equal portions.

Shape each portion into a desired shape, such as rolls or a loaf. Place the shaped dough on a baking sheet lined with parchment paper.

Cover the dough with a clean kitchen towel and let it rise for another 30-45 minutes until puffed.

Preheat the oven to 350°F (175°C).

Brush the risen dough with the egg wash.

Bake in the preheated oven for about 20-25 minutes until golden brown and baked through.

The Asian kitchen

Remove from the oven and let the bread cool on a wire rack before slicing and serving.

Enjoy the spicy and flavorful Chinese Mapo Tofu and the soft and fluffy Japanese Milk Bread from "The Asian Kitchen: A Delightful Collection of Chinese, Korean, and Baking Bread Recipes for Your Family Cookbook." Happy cooking and baking!

The Asian kitchen

Chinese Egg Fried Rice:

Ingredients:

2 cups cooked jasmine rice, chilled

2 tablespoons vegetable oil

2 cloves garlic, minced

1/2 cup frozen peas and carrots, thawed

2 eggs, lightly beaten

2 tablespoons soy sauce

1 tablespoon oyster sauce (optional)

2 green onions, chopped

Salt and pepper to taste

Preparation:

Heat vegetable oil in a wok or large skillet over medium-high heat.

Add minced garlic to the hot oil and stir-fry for about 1 minute until fragrant.

The Asian kitchen

Add frozen peas and carrots to the wok and stir-fry for 2-3 minutes until heated through.

Push the vegetables to one side of the wok and pour the beaten eggs into the empty side. Scramble the eggs until cooked.

Add the chilled jasmine rice to the wok and stir-fry with the vegetables and eggs, breaking up any clumps.

Drizzle soy sauce and oyster sauce (if using) over the rice. Stir-fry for another 2-3 minutes until well combined and heated through.

Season with salt and pepper to taste.

Remove from heat and garnish with chopped green onions. Serve hot as a

The Asian kitchen

delicious and quick Chinese-inspired fried rice.

Korean Kimchi Pancakes (Kimchijeon):

Ingredients:

1 cup all-purpose flour

1 cup kimchi, drained and chopped

1/2 cup kimchi juice

1/4 cup water

2 green onions, chopped

2 tablespoons vegetable oil

Dipping sauce:

2 tablespoons soy sauce

1 tablespoon rice vinegar

1 teaspoon sesame oil

The Asian kitchen

1 teaspoon sesame seeds

Preparation:

In a large bowl, combine all-purpose flour, chopped kimchi, kimchi juice, water, and chopped green onions. Mix well until a thick batter forms.

Heat vegetable oil in a skillet or frying pan over medium heat.

Scoop a ladleful of the kimchi batter onto the hot skillet and spread it out into a circular shape.

Cook the pancake for about 2-3 minutes on each side until golden brown and crispy.

Transfer the cooked pancake to a plate lined with paper towels to remove excess oil.

Repeat the process with the remaining batter to make more pancakes.

The Asian kitchen

In a small bowl, whisk together soy sauce, rice vinegar, sesame oil, and sesame seeds to make the dipping sauce.

Cut the kimchi pancakes into wedges and serve hot with the dipping sauce on the side.

Enjoy the savory Chinese Egg Fried Rice and the flavorful Korean Kimchi Pancakes from "The Asian Kitchen: A Delightful Collection of Chinese, Korean, and Baking Bread Recipes for Your Family Cookbook." Happy cooking and enjoy your meal!

The Asian kitchen

Chinese Kung Pao Chicken:

Ingredients:

1 lb (450g) boneless, skinless chicken breasts, cut into small cubes

1/2 cup unsalted peanuts

1 red bell pepper, diced

1 green bell pepper, diced

1/2 cup diced onion

3 cloves garlic, minced

2 tablespoons vegetable oil

2 tablespoons soy sauce

1 tablespoon hoisin sauce

1 tablespoon rice vinegar

1 tablespoon cornstarch, dissolved in 2 tablespoons water

1 teaspoon sugar

1 teaspoon Sichuan peppercorns, crushed (optional for extra heat)

Salt to taste

The Asian kitchen

Cooked rice, for serving

In a small bowl, whisk together soy sauce, hoisin sauce, rice vinegar, cornstarch-water mixture, sugar, and crushed Sichuan peppercorns (if using). Set aside.

Heat vegetable oil in a wok or large skillet over high heat.

Add diced chicken to the hot oil and stir-fry for about 5-6 minutes until browned and cooked through. Remove the chicken from the wok and set aside.

In the same wok, add minced garlic and diced onion. Stir-fry for about 1 minute until fragrant and slightly softened.

The Asian kitchen

Add diced bell peppers to the wok and stir-fry for another 2-3 minutes until crisp-tender.

Return the cooked chicken to the wok and pour the sauce mixture over the ingredients. Stir-fry for another 1-2 minutes until the sauce thickens and coats the chicken and vegetables.

Stir in the unsalted peanuts and cook for an additional minute.

Taste the dish and season with salt if needed.

Remove from heat and serve hot over cooked rice for a delicious and spicy Chinese Kung Pao Chicken.

The Asian kitchen

Korean Japchae (Stir-Fried Glass Noodles with Vegetables):

Ingredients:

8 oz (225g) sweet potato glass noodles (dangmyeon)

2 tablespoons vegetable oil, divided

2 cloves garlic, minced

1/2 cup sliced carrots

1/2 cup sliced bell peppers

1/2 cup sliced mushrooms (shiitake or button mushrooms)

1/2 cup sliced onions

2 cups spinach

2 tablespoons soy sauce

1 tablespoon sesame oil

1 tablespoon sugar

2 green onions, chopped

The Asian kitchen

Toasted sesame seeds, for garnish

Cook the sweet potato glass noodles according to the package instructions. Drain and set aside.

Heat 1 tablespoon of vegetable oil in a large skillet or wok over medium heat.

Add minced garlic and sliced carrots to the hot oil and stir-fry for about 2 minutes until the carrots begin to soften.

Add sliced bell peppers, mushrooms, and onions to the skillet. Continue to stir-fry for another 3-4 minutes until the vegetables are crisp-tender.

Push the vegetables to one side of the skillet and add the remaining 1 tablespoon of vegetable oil to the empty side. Add the spinach to the hot oil and stir-fry until wilted.

The Asian kitchen

Combine the cooked glass noodles, stir-fried vegetables, and spinach in the skillet. Mix well.

In a small bowl, whisk together soy sauce, sesame oil, and sugar. Pour the sauce over the noodles and vegetables. Stir-fry for another 2-3 minutes until the noodles are evenly coated and heated through.

Remove from heat and garnish with chopped green onions and toasted sesame seeds.

Serve hot as a flavorful and satisfying Korean Japchae.

Enjoy the spicy and flavorful Chinese Kung Pao Chicken and the delicious Korean Japchae from "The Asian Kitchen: A Delightful Collection of Chinese, Korean, and Baking Bread Recipes for Your Family Cookbook." Happy cooking and enjoy your meal!

Chinese Steamed Dumplings (Jiaozi):

Ingredients:

For the filling:

1 lb (450g) ground pork

1 cup finely chopped Napa cabbage

2 green onions, finely chopped

2 cloves garlic, minced

1 tablespoon grated ginger

1 tablespoon soy sauce

1 tablespoon sesame oil

1/2 teaspoon salt

1/4 teaspoon black pepper

For the dumpling wrappers:

2 cups all-purpose flour

1 cup water

Additional flour for dusting

The Asian kitchen

Preparation:

In a large bowl, combine ground pork, Napa cabbage, green onions, minced garlic, grated ginger, soy sauce, sesame oil, salt, and black pepper. Mix well until all the ingredients are evenly incorporated.

In a separate bowl, mix all-purpose flour and water until a soft dough forms.

Transfer the dough to a lightly floured surface and knead for about 5 minutes until smooth and elastic. Cover with a damp cloth and let it rest for 30 minutes.

Roll out the dough into a thin sheet and use a round cookie cutter or glass to cut out circles of about 3-4 inches in diameter.

The Asian kitchen

Place a spoonful of the filling in the center of each dumpling wrapper. Fold the wrapper in half and pinch the edges to seal, creating a half-moon shape.

Repeat the process until all the filling and wrappers are used.

Prepare a steamer and line it with parchment paper or cabbage leaves to prevent sticking.

Arrange the dumplings in the steamer, leaving some space between each dumpling to prevent sticking.

Steam the dumplings for about 12-15 minutes until cooked through.

Remove from the steamer and serve hot with your choice of dipping sauce, such as soy sauce or vinegar-based sauce.

The Asian kitchen

Baking Bread: Chinese BBQ Pork Buns (Char Siu Bao):

Ingredients:

For the dough:

3 cups all-purpose flour

1/4 cup granulated sugar

1 tablespoon active dry yeast

1/2 teaspoon salt

1 cup warm milk

2 tablespoons vegetable oil

For the filling:

1 cup Chinese BBQ pork (Char Siu), diced

2 tablespoons hoisin sauce

1 tablespoon soy sauce

1 tablespoon oyster sauce

The Asian kitchen

1 tablespoon cornstarch, dissolved in 2 tablespoons water

Preparation:

In a large bowl, combine all-purpose flour, granulated sugar, active dry yeast, and salt. Mix well.

Add warm milk and vegetable oil to the bowl. Stir until a soft dough forms.

Transfer the dough to a lightly floured surface and knead for about 10 minutes until smooth and elastic.

Place the dough in a greased bowl, cover with a clean kitchen towel, and let it rise in a warm place for about 1 hour or until doubled in size.

Punch down the dough and turn it out onto a lightly floured surface. Divide the dough into equal portions.

Flatten each dough portion into a circle and place a spoonful of the filling in the center.

The Asian kitchen

Gather the edges of the dough and pinch them together to seal, creating a ball-shaped bun.

Place the filled buns on a baking sheet lined with parchment paper, leaving some space between each bun.

Let the buns rest for another 30 minutes to rise.

Preheat the oven to 350°F (180°C).

Bake the buns for about 15-18 minutes until golden brown.

Remove from the oven and let them cool for a few minutes before serving.

Enjoy the savory Chinese Steamed Dumplings (Jiaozi) and the delightful Chinese BBQ Pork Buns (Char Siu Bao) from "The Asian Kitchen: A Delightful Collection of Chinese, Korean, and Baking Bread Recipes for Your Family Cookbook." Happy cooking and enjoy your meal!

Chinese Hot and Sour Soup:

Ingredients:

4 cups chicken or vegetable broth

1/2 cup sliced mushrooms (shiitake or button mushrooms)

1/4 cup bamboo shoots, thinly sliced

1/4 cup firm tofu, diced

2 tablespoons soy sauce

2 tablespoons rice vinegar

1 tablespoon cornstarch, dissolved in 2 tablespoons water

1 egg, beaten

2 green onions, thinly sliced

1/2 teaspoon sesame oil

Salt and pepper to taste

Preparation:

The Asian kitchen

In a large pot, bring the chicken or vegetable broth to a boil.

Add sliced mushrooms, bamboo shoots, and diced tofu to the pot. Simmer for about 5 minutes until the vegetables are tender.

In a small bowl, mix together soy sauce, rice vinegar, and cornstarch-water mixture to create a slurry.

Pour the slurry into the pot and stir well. Allow the soup to thicken for a few minutes.

Slowly drizzle the beaten egg into the pot while stirring the soup gently in a circular motion. This will create ribbons of cooked egg in the soup.

The Asian kitchen

Add sliced green onions and sesame oil to the soup. Stir to combine.

Season with salt and pepper to taste.

Remove from heat and serve hot as a comforting and flavorful Chinese Hot and Sour Soup.

The Asian kitchen

Korean Bulgogi:

Ingredients:

1 lb (450g) beef sirloin, thinly sliced

1/4 cup soy sauce

2 tablespoons sesame oil

2 tablespoons brown sugar

2 cloves garlic, minced

1 tablespoon grated ginger

1 tablespoon rice vinegar

1 tablespoon vegetable oil

1/2 onion, thinly sliced

2 green onions, sliced

Sesame seeds, for garnish

Cooked rice, for serving

Preparation:

The Asian kitchen

In a bowl, whisk together soy sauce, sesame oil, brown sugar, minced garlic, grated ginger, and rice vinegar to create a marinade.

Add the thinly sliced beef to the marinade and toss until well coated. Allow the beef to marinate for at least 30 minutes or up to 2 hours in the refrigerator.

Heat vegetable oil in a large skillet or wok over high heat.

Add the sliced onion to the hot oil and stir-fry for about 2 minutes until softened.

Add the marinated beef to the skillet and stir-fry for 4-5 minutes until the beef is cooked through and slightly caramelized.

Add the sliced green onions to the skillet and cook for another minute.

Remove from heat and garnish with sesame seeds.

Serve hot over cooked rice for a delicious and flavorful Korean Bulgogi.

The Asian kitchen

Enjoy the comforting Chinese Hot and Sour Soup and the flavorful Korean Bulgogi from "The Asian Kitchen: A Delightful Collection of Chinese, Korean, and Baking Bread Recipes for Your Family Cookbook." Happy cooking and enjoy your meal!

Chinese Dim Sum: Shumai (Steamed Dumplings):

Ingredients:

1/2 lb (225g) ground pork

1/2 lb (225g) shrimp, peeled and deveined

1/4 cup finely chopped water chestnuts

2 tablespoons finely chopped green onions

1 tablespoon soy sauce

1 tablespoon sesame oil

The Asian kitchen

1 tablespoon cornstarch

1 teaspoon grated ginger

1/2 teaspoon sugar

1/4 teaspoon white pepper

24 round dumpling wrappers

Green peas or carrot slices for garnish

Preparation:

In a food processor, pulse the shrimp until finely chopped. Transfer to a large bowl.

Add ground pork, water chestnuts, green onions, soy sauce, sesame oil, cornstarch, grated ginger, sugar, and white pepper to the bowl with the shrimp. Mix well until all the ingredients are combined.

Place a tablespoon of the filling in the center of each dumpling wrapper.

The Asian kitchen

Gather the edges of the wrapper and pleat to form a small cup-shaped dumpling. Leave the top exposed.

Place the dumplings on a steamer lined with parchment paper or cabbage leaves.

Garnish each dumpling with a green pea or carrot slice.

Steam the dumplings for about 12-15 minutes until cooked through.

Remove from the steamer and serve hot with your favorite dipping sauce, such as soy sauce or chili sauce.

The Asian kitchen

Korean Kimchi Fried Rice:

Ingredients:

2 cups cooked rice, preferably day-old rice

1 cup kimchi, chopped

1/2 cup diced cooked chicken or pork (optional)

1/4 cup diced carrots

1/4 cup frozen peas

2 cloves garlic, minced

2 tablespoons soy sauce

1 tablespoon sesame oil

1 tablespoon vegetable oil

2 green onions, sliced

1 tablespoon toasted sesame seeds

Fried eggs, for serving (optional)

Preparation:

The Asian kitchen

Heat vegetable oil in a large skillet or wok over medium heat.

Add minced garlic and diced carrots to the hot oil and stir-fry for about 2 minutes until the carrots start to soften.

Add diced chicken or pork (if using) to the skillet and cook for an additional 2 minutes.

Add chopped kimchi and frozen peas to the skillet. Stir-fry for another 2-3 minutes until heated through.

Add cooked rice to the skillet and stir-fry for 3-4 minutes, breaking up any clumps.

In a small bowl, whisk together soy sauce and sesame oil. Pour the sauce over the rice mixture and stir well to combine.

Add sliced green onions and toasted sesame seeds to the skillet. Stir-fry for another minute.

Remove from heat and serve hot. Top each serving with a fried egg, if desired.

Enjoy the delicious Chinese Dim Sum: Shumai and the flavorful Korean Kimchi

The Asian kitchen

Fried Rice from "The Asian Kitchen: A Delightful Collection of Chinese, Korean, and Baking Bread Recipes for Your Family Cookbook." Happy cooking and enjoy your meal!

The Asian kitchen

In conclusion

"The Asian Kitchen: A Delightful Collection of Chinese, Korean, and Baking Bread Recipes for Your Family Cookbook" offers a diverse array of mouthwatering recipes that will delight your taste buds and bring the flavors of Asia into your home. From traditional Chinese favorites to authentic Korean dishes, this cookbook is a treasure trove of culinary delights.

Whether you're a seasoned cook or just starting your culinary journey, this cookbook provides clear and easy-to-follow instructions for each recipe, ensuring that you can recreate the flavors and aromas of Asian cuisine with confidence. The recipes feature a variety of ingredients that can be easily found in local supermarkets, making them accessible to cooks of all levels.

The Asian kitchen

From the savory Chinese Kung Pao Chicken to the comforting Korean Bulgogi, each dish is thoughtfully crafted to capture the essence of Asian cooking. The book also includes a selection of baking bread recipes, adding a delightful twist to your culinary repertoire.

Moreover, this cookbook emphasizes the importance of family and the joy of cooking together. The recipes are designed to be shared and enjoyed with loved ones, creating memorable experiences and fostering a sense of togetherness in the kitchen.

"The Asian Kitchen" is not only a collection of recipes but also a cultural journey, as it provides insights into the culinary traditions and techniques that have shaped Asian cuisine. It celebrates the rich flavors, vibrant colors, and diverse ingredients that make Asian cooking so captivating.

The Asian kitchen

So, whether you're craving the bold flavors of Chinese cuisine, the spicy delights of Korean dishes, or the comforting aroma of freshly baked bread, "The Asian Kitchen" is your go-to guide. It invites you to embark on a culinary adventure and explore the flavors of Asia in the comfort of your own kitchen.

Get ready to tantalize your taste buds, impress your family and friends, and create unforgettable culinary experiences with the recipes from "The Asian Kitchen: A Delightful Collection of Chinese, Korean, and Baking Bread Recipes for Your Family Cookbook." Happy cooking!

The Asian kitchen

Printed in Great Britain
by Amazon

25753947R00056